72 Hour Product

Create an Outrageously Profitable Information Product in Only 72 Hours

By Scott Brooks

Printed in the United States of America.
First Printing: June 2010
ISBN - 1453600353

Preface

This idea for this book was birthed out of personal frustration and need. The length of time it took me to research and create an information product from start to finish was just too time-consuming and unsatisfying.

Since every internet marketer's success is based on his ability to create and implement proven systems, I knew that I needed to create a good system for cranking out information products quickly.

I meticulously analyzed the information product creation process, looking for the fastest and most effective solutions for each step. I put the pieces together and tested the process thoroughly.

It is my desire that the system outlined in the book will be a valuable resource for new internet marketers as well as seasoned veterans. Enjoy!

Acknowledgements

I am very grateful to my wife for her patience with me while I researched and created this book. She understood and supported my vision for this project.

Thanks also to Trevor Lund for creating the beautiful cover for this book. Trevor is an incredibly talented individual who possesses expertise in several areas. Please visit his website at: www.AskandImagine.com.

Contents

1

PREPARATION

Introduction

Congratulations on purchasing this book. Although this comprehensive guide will provide you with all the information you need to produce quality, in-demand information products, it will require a great deal of self-discipline and attention to detail on your part. In this chapter I will cover a couple essential tasks you will need to implement before you begin the process of creating your own information products.

Prepare Your Mind

One of the greatest challenges many new internet marketers face is the ability to maintain focus. Let's be honest, you can indeed create an information product from scratch in 72 hours or less; however, you will need to have a laser-type focus and not allow yourself to become distracted.

If you constantly feel the need to check your emails, social networking profile, or watch your favorite TV shows, you'll need to change your mindset and lifestyle before attempting this endeavor. Otherwise, you'll drag this process on and on and will more than likely never finish your product. This endeavor <u>WILL</u> require sacrifice, but if you do it right, the payoff will be well worth it.

The good news is that you only need 72 *good* hours to complete this product. You can do this! Make a list of those things that distract you and determine to limit or eliminate them completely during this process. Now if you are like me, I need to check my emails daily since it's the primary method I use to communicate.

In this case, it is important to schedule a specific time during the day to check and respond to your emails and to do those tasks during this allotted time *only*.

Create a Schedule

There's an old saying, "If you don't manage your time, everyone else will do it for you". Isn't this true? When we don't manage our valuable time by creating and adhering to a schedule, other people and circumstances control our lives.

The next vital step during the preparation phase is to block out the 72 hours needed to begin and complete your product. Don't make the mistake of blocking out an hour here and an hour there because you increase the chances of becoming distracted and discouraged.

If you have a full-time job then you'll need to see when you can schedule the largest blocks of time. For example, if you work a 9-5 job, set a few hours aside each evening to work on your product. If you block out three good hours each evening Monday thru Friday and nine hours on Saturday, you will have your product completed in three weeks or less.

To be totally honest with you, after you get this process down, you will be able to create products in much less time than 72 hours - even if you have a full-time job.
I can easily create a full eBook in a week or less, but I've had a lot of practice.

Imagine cranking out two or three hot-selling products each month! It can be done and once you get the hang of it, it's really not too hard. The key is to develop a system that works. That's the purpose of this book.

OK, lets not get ahead of ourselves. We need to focus on just one product right now - the first one! Lets dive in, shall we?

2

BRAINSTORMING

Choosing a Niche

When selling a product, many people make the mistake of developing their product first and then trying to find or create a market for it. The process should be reversed. Find a market first that spends money, find out what they want, and then sell it to them.

People will pay good money for information that answers a burning question, relieves their pain or solves a problem.

One of the best places to get hot product ideas is eBay Pulse (http://pulse.ebay.com). This nifty tool provides a daily snapshot of their top searches, which is incredible considering the fact that practically everyone conducting searches on eBay is looking to *buy*. To use eBay pulse, simply click on the drop down menu and select a niche – one in which you find interesting and/or possess some degree of knowledge. You'll then see a list of the top ten categories for that search.

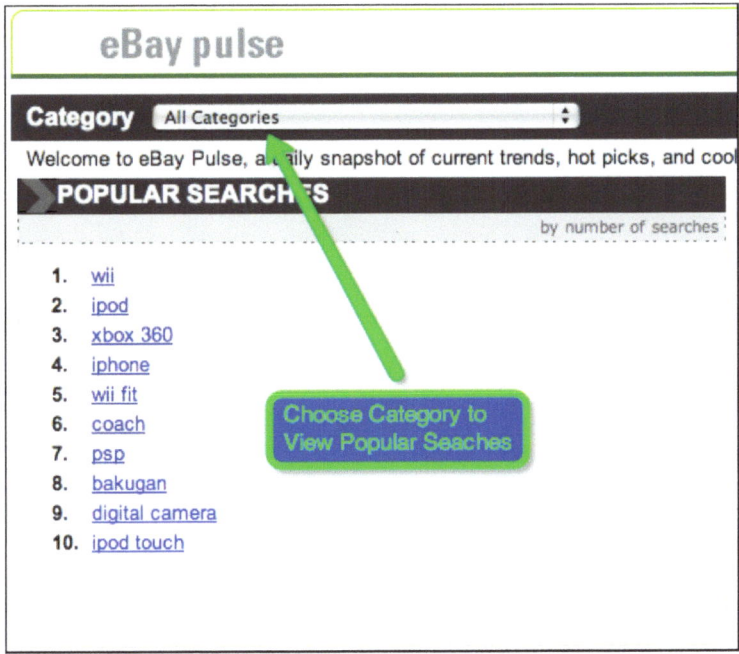

Dig deeper by clicking on the category drop down menu. In the image below, I first selected "Business & Industrial." Then, I selected "Businesses and Websites for Sale." Finally, I selected "Internet Businesses and Websites" which is the last subcategory under the "Business & Industrial" category.

I noticed that "traffic" showed up under both subcategories. This tells me that many consumers are conducting searches for products related to website traffic.

A very important thing to keep in mind is that most consumers surfing eBay are looking to buy "physical products" instead of "digital products" such as eBooks; however, practically everyone desires information. Therefore, when we need or want to learn about something, we search for information to fulfill that desire. There is good reason to believe that an information product on practically any niche would sell if the demand were there.

OK, back to our brainstorming session. You can dig even deeper by clicking on "traffic." After the new page loads, take a look down the left-hand side and click on "completed items". This will display a list of items that have sold under the "traffic" category.

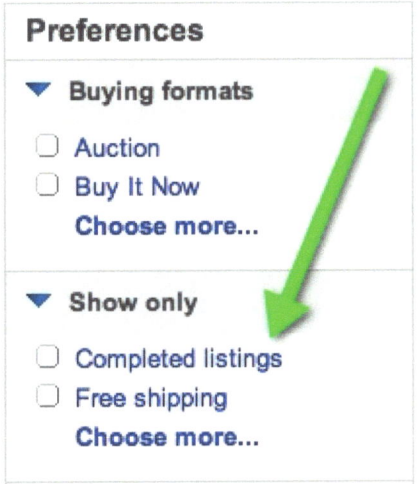

At this point eBay Pulse has told us two very important things about the niche, "traffic".

1. People are looking for information on website traffic.

2. People are buying products related to website traffic.

Now, we need to do a little research to determine if a product created about website traffic would be profitable.

As I walk through this process in the next chapter, please keep in mind that regardless of the niche, the steps are the same. Therefore, this procedure will work for any niche idea you have.

3

MARKET RESEARCH

Step One: Harvesting Keywords

Now we need to harvest a list of keywords to look for sub-niches related to "website traffic" (i.e. methods for acquiring website traffic) and determine the demand and current level of competition in this niche.

We could use a keyword tool to conduct this research, but I've recently discovered a new free tool created by called PPC Web Spy. This tool displays keywords used by Google ads. This is a nifty little tool because other marketers have already done the research for you. How cool is that? You can download this powerful free tool here: www.ppcwebspy.com.

Let's go to PPC Spy and look for keywords related to "website traffic". To perform this task, we'll go to Google and type "traffic" into the search field. We then need to click on "View Keywords" for every ad and harvest the keywords related to the niche "website traffic". Some of the keywords displayed will be totally unrelated, so just ignore them and harvest the relevant ones.

The screenshot below displays keywords used by one of the ads. In this particular ad there are three keywords that are highly targeted to our main keyword, "website traffic".

After we've harvested a list of keywords related to "website traffic" from all ads, we then need to rinse and repeat by performing the same process using each of the keywords we've initially harvested. We'll do this until we've harvested at least 50 relevant keywords.

This process is grueling and time-consuming as you might imagine, but it will certainly help us determine if creating a product on "website traffic" is worth the time and effort. It will also give us plenty of keywords we can use to promote this product, which will save valuable time later.

Step Two: Analyzing Keywords

To analyze keywords, we'll use Google's Traffic Estimator

(h t t p s : / / a d w o r d s . g o o g l e . c o m / s e l e c t / TrafficEstimatorSandbox). We'll also open Google's search engine in a new tab to find out the number of competing sites (the organic competition) for each keyword we select.

During this process, we'll analyze the keywords to find a narrow niche in which:

- People are looking for related products to buy.
- The market is not too saturated already.
- There is not much free information available.

First, we need to paste the keywords that we've harvested from PPC Spy into Google's Traffic Estimator. Leave the other fields blank except for the "country" field at the bottom.

After clicking "continue," we see that many of our keywords are getting decent traffic, which is a good thing.

Maximum CPC:	Daily budget:	Get New Estimates
Keywords	Search Volume ▼	Estimated Avg. CPC
Search Network Total		$4.27 - $5.67
online advertising		$4.81 - $6.18
business advertising		$3.57 - $5.36
home based business marketing		$4.04 - $5.38
get web traffic		$6.80 - $8.52
free advertisement		$1.55 - $2.03
free internet marketing		$3.68 - $4.72
free business advertising		$2.80 - $4.20
free online marketing		$4.25 - $5.32
purchase traffic		$3.47 - $4.34
free marketing ideas		$2.10 - $2.77
free trade leads		$0.80 - $1.01
free home business advertising		$3.19 - $4.79
promoting your website		$8.02 - $10.22
free ezine ads		$1.12 - $1.40
web site traffic report		$4.62 - $6.93

Some of the pay per click ads are a bit pricey, but this means products related to "website traffic" are selling because people are buying ads.

Google's CPC (cost per click) is for the top ad position, so clicks will be significantly cheaper than what they're reporting, especially if the ads and sales letter are well optimized.

Now, we'll paste our keywords into a spreadsheet. At the bottom of Traffic Estimator's results page you will see the button "Download as .csv". Clicking this button will download the results and format them into a spreadsheet. Keeping an analysis of all your keywords is vital.

At this point, we need to look over our list of keywords to find a common theme. We can't create a generic product on "website traffic," because it's just too nonspecific and broad. Let's look over our keywords to find a related theme.

One thing I notice right off is that many of these keywords contain the word "free" which is not surprising since advertisers are always looking to save money on getting traffic to their sites.

A keyword that catches my eye on the list is "free advertising on the internet".

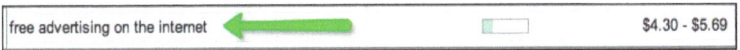

If we decide to create a product on how to get free website traffic, this looks like a good niche. This keyword generates low traffic in the search engines; however, there are many additional, relevant keywords that can be used to promote our product and this will result in significant traffic. Lets analyze it further.

We'll now assess the competition for "free advertising on the internet". To perform this action, we'll open Google's search engine, then type our keyword in the search field using quotation marks.

Using quotation marks around our keyword will produce the number of competing sites; this will indicate how a site promoted using this keyword will perform in the search engines.

If there are too many competing sites, this means the niche is too competitive. If there are few competing pages, there's a chance that a site promoted using this keyword (free advertising on the internet) might do well.

The image below displays the number of competing pages for the keyword "free advertising on the internet".

As you can see from the image above, there are 9,670 competing pages for this keyword. This sounds like a large number; however, considering that there are billions of web pages, it's a relatively small amount. In fact, I am comfortable advertising with keywords that have 20,000 or less competing pages.

Another promising fact is that there are several ads promoting products or services using this keyword, so this tells us that there is money in this niche.

MARKET RESEARCH

Step Three: Analyzing the Competition

Now, there is another important factor to consider - the level of competition from both free and paid sites. If there is already a wealth of free information on this keyword or if there is an abundance of paid services or products, it obviously means the competition for this keyword is too stiff, and it would be futile to create a product around this keyword.

To check out the competition, we'll simply look at some of the sites on Google's first page by typing our main keyword into Google's search engine without quotation marks.

The results are quite promising. Most of the sites we analyzed are advertising classified ad services or a specific type of advertising.

Since we've decided to create a product on how to advertise on the internet using a variety of methods, this is good news!

I believe that many people who type, "free advertising on the internet" into Google are looking for more than just one free advertising method.

4

THE DOMAIN NAME

Now that we've found what looks to be a promising keyword to target as a niche for our product, we need to select a domain name. There are two schools of thought when it comes to selecting a domain name.

Choosing a Domain Name for Branding

The first school of thought is to select a domain name that it is catchy and descriptive in order to brand a product or service. This domain is usually not a keyword and is used to describe the product and entice consumers to buy. Branding is often used by well-established marketers who have large lists of subscribers and who are planning to use others to promote their product (i.e., affiliates and JV partners).

A good example of branding is the title of this eBook. I certainly don't consider myself a big-time marketer; however, when planning this project my strategy was to use an army of affiliates and JV partners.

Choosing a Keyword Domain Name

Since search engines place some emphasis on domain names when ranking sites, using a keyword-rich domain name is advantageous, especially if it is highly relevant to the product or service being promoted.

For our product, we'll use a keyword phrase for our domain name. Since we've decided to create a product on the niche "free advertising on the internet", we'll check to find out if this domain name is available.

The .com domain is what we're after, not because there would be an advantage in search engine rankings, but rather because most web surfers view .com websites as being the most legitimate.

Our second choice would be a .net. Some internet marketers believe that certain domain extensions (.com, .net, .info, etc.) rank better than others, but my experience has proven this theory to be false. I've had several .info sites rank very well. Honestly, it's simply a matter of a website's content and the quality and quantity of backlinks a site has that determines it's ranking.

To find out if our domain name is available, we'll use Godaddy.com. There are many other places you can buy domain names, so if you have a company you prefer to use, go for it.

After looking up freeadvertisingontheinternet.com, we see that it's not available. Bummer! All hope is not lost, though. We can also check the availability of this domain using hyphens between the words. There isn't any harm in doing this. In fact, some website owners prefer domain names that are hyphenated, because they are easier to read.

Some folks may argue that a long domain name is harder to type in a browser. This is true, but seriously, how many people are going to type a long-tail domain name in their browser anyway?

Besides, our goal should be to generate traffic to our sales letter and this domain with hyphens should help to do this. OK, this domain is available.

Congratulations! You've completed the most difficult part of this process. Give yourself a pat on the back! The rest of the product creation process is hard work, but it is also fun and rewarding.

At this point I think it's important to point out that you do not have to create a product in the internet marketing niche. In fact, this is one of the more competitive niches. There are literally hundreds of niches that are virtually untapped, so use your creativity and imagination to choose a niche that you believe will make you money and one that interests you.

5

PRODUCT CREATION OVERVIEW

In this chapter, I will provide two methods for creating information products: the research method and the interview method. Lets take a look at the pros and cons of each method.

Overview of the Research Method

This is the "old school" method of conducting research to find information. This process is similar to the one that ghostwriters use to write content. It's the reason these writers can produce content on virtually any topic in a relatively quick manner. The advantage this method affords is the ability to have total control over the content. The disadvantage is obviously the time and effort required to find useful, relative content in order to create a quality product. Choosing a niche in which you have some degree of knowledge is certainly advantageous and will expedite this process significantly.

Overview of the Interview Method

This method involves interviewing an expert or experts. The interview is recorded and packaged as an MP3, CD, transcribed text or a combination of the three. This method has several advantages, one of which is the simplicity and ease of producing a quality information product. Another advantage of the interview method is the ability to charge more since the information is from an expert. This is certainly dependent on how well known and well respected the expert is in his or her field.

The interview method has become quite popular mainly because one can crank out a quality product very quickly.

One disadvantage of this method, if you want to think of it that way, is the time and trouble required to locate an expert that has substantial knowledge on the topic and has time to be interviewed.

If you decide to use this method, you may be surprised at how willing many experts are to be interviewed. The reason is because these individuals like the exposure and understand the profit potential involved with these endeavors.

6

CREATING THE OUTLINE

Now we'll walk through the process of creating an outline for our product. The outline is simply a list of sections or chapters and provides us with the "big picture" of what our information product will look like. Since we've decided to produce a product on the niche "free advertising on the internet," we need to decide what free advertisement methods we'll cover in our product. I know of several free advertising methods on which we could produce information, but we need to work through the process on the premise that we know nothing about this niche. Therefore, we must find out what we can produce content around.

Where is the best place to get answers to questions on the internet? There are several good places, one of which is Yahoo Answers (http://answers.yahoo.com). This is a great resource that provides answers to practically any question you can think of.

Let's go ask Yahoo Answers about types of free advertising on the internet.

After typing "free advertising on the internet," we see there are 561 answers. Wow! Lets go through a few of these to try to find content we can use to create our outline.

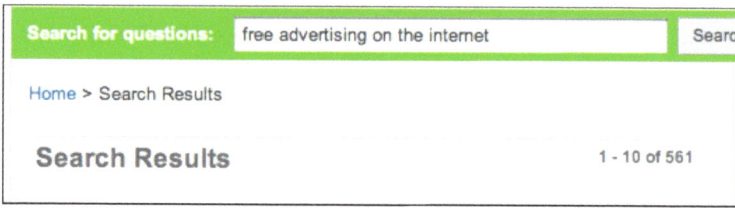

Now, we need to keep in mind that people who answer questions on Yahoo Answers are sharing their opinions and some are also blatant advertisements. However, with a little discernment, we'll be able to find legitimate information.

Let's attempt to find at least 15 "free advertising on the internet" methods that we can produce content around.

Yahoo Answers may also provide us with additional, valuable information about free advertising sources, so it would be a good idea to record this information and bookmark sites recommended by Yahoo Answers users who are providing answers. This will save us valuable time when we begin to produce the content for our information product.

After researching Yahoo Answers, we've compiled our list of 15 possible topics on which we can produce information on free advertising on the internet.

CREATING THE OUTLINE

```
Forums
Social Networking Sites
Social Bookmarking Sites
Article Marketing
Blog Comments
Classified Ads
Affiliate Marketing
Blogging
Search Engine Optimization
Video Marketing
Link Exchanges
Press Releases
Directories
Traffic Exchanges
Viral Ebooks
```

7

THE RESEARCH METHOD
FOR CREATING CONTENT

Answering The Two Key Questions

It's important to keep in mind that consumers who buy information products are looking for a quick answer to a question or a solution to a problem. To give customers what they need, we must put ourselves in their place.

This is quite simple because there are always two key questions we can answer, regardless of the niche, to give consumers what they need: the "what" and the "how". For example, if someone is looking for weight-loss information, their bottom-line question may be "how can I lose weight", but they really need to know *what* to do and *how* to do it. That's it! Isn't this simple? Think about it. This is true with any niche you choose.

In the case with our niche, "free advertising on the

internet," we need to answer two questions: *"what* are the best free advertising methods on the internet?" and *"how* do I use them?"

In this step, we'll walk through the steps involved in creating content on each of our 15 "free advertising on the internet" processes.

We're getting close! In this section, we'll conduct research and create content on one of our advertising methods to see how this process works. Let's go with "Press Releases".

Using Websites to Conduct Research

There are many great websites we can use for conducting research including the one we just used to compile our list of free advertising methods, Yahoo Answers. Below are a few other great sites for conducting research.

Wikipedia.com
Nearly every web surfer knows about this online encyclopedia, which contains information on nearly any topic. Since the general public posts information, there are occasional inaccuracies in content; however, the site is monitored closely and these inaccuracies are rare.

About.com
Great site where you can find accurate answers to almost any question. They even include a promise to provide readers with accurate, engaging content.

Gistweb.com
This little known site is my favorite place to go when I need a great deal of content. Each search pulls information from sources all over the internet, and they are

divided by paragraphs. Each paragraph ends with a hyperlinked reference number, so users can quickly access the original source with one click.

Before we begin conducting research on "press releases," let's create a list of search terms. We need to consider our two key questions when conducting this research, the *what* and *how*.

We also need to keep in mind that our ultimate goal is to instruct our readers about how press releases can be used as a free adverting tool. Compiling this list will ensure that our research produces targeted, relevant information.

Here are a few keyword phrases we can use when conducting research:

- writing press releases
- best free press release sites
- advertise using press releases

OK, how 'bout we give this research thing a shot? First, we'll go to my favorite research site, Gistweb.com, and use their *summaries* feature. Now, I must inform you that Gistweb's summaries only work with Internet Explorer, which is a bummer for hardcore Macintosh users like myself.

Therefore, if you plan to use Gistweb.com for conducting research, and I highly recommend that you do, then you'll need to get your hands on a PC; however, this shouldn't be too difficult. You can get free access to a PC at your local library or borrow one from a friend or relative. My wife lets me borrow her PC if I reciprocate by cooking her a good meal or cleaning the bathrooms! You can conduct the research, copy and paste into an email, and send it to yourself.

THE RESEARCH METHOD FOR CREATING CONTENT

After typing "writing press releases" in Gistweb's search field, we need to select three other fields: *source, summary length* and *algorithm*. I personally think it's a good idea to try them all since each one will harvest different information.

Important: The information on Gistweb and/or any other source should be used for research purposes only. You need to study the information, then write your own, unique content. Don't steal other people's work!

Use the same process you would if you were writing a college research paper.

After randomly selecting the fields *Web, Medium* and *GistPro*, then pressing the "Gist the Web" button, it appears that we've found some very valuable research (see image below). We'll simply copy and paste the information that we deem to be valuable and relevant into a text document.

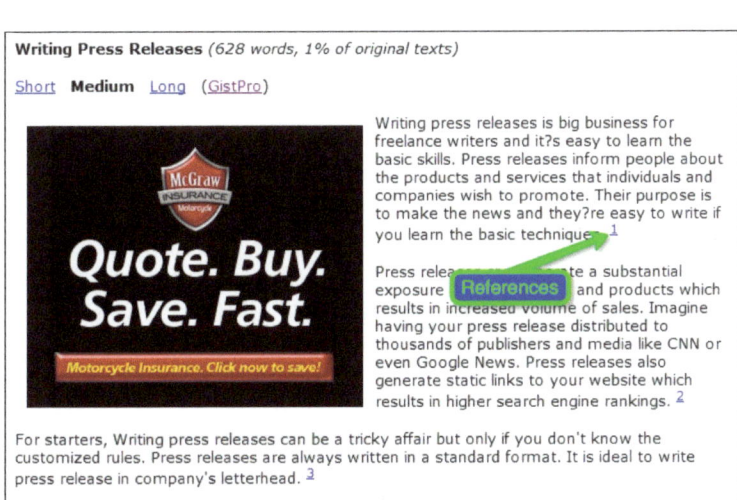

Now, we just need to repeat this process with Gistweb, selecting each of the other fields (i.e., *News, Long, GistLite,* etc.). Also, we must repeat this process with our other keyword phrases: *advertise using press releases* and *best press release sites.*

Since Gistweb primarily harvests web content in paragraph form, we'll most likely need to visit a few other research sites to access our list of the best press release sites.
To get a good list of press release sites, let's head over to Yahoo Answers. These sites should have the information we need.

After typing the keyword phrase "best press release sites" in Yahoo Answers, we see that there are over 300 results! Thankfully, Yahoo sorts the most relevant results at the beginning.

After looking at a few of the threads on Yahoo Answers, we'll compile a list of these sites. Then, we can check out other sources to cross-reference our findings and locate additional free press release sites.

We can look on Wikipedia, About.com, or we can simply conduct a good old-fashioned web search. Let's try that.

After typing "free press release sites" using quotation marks in Google, we find much relevant information on free press release sites. Wow! Look at all these results:

THE RESEARCH METHOD FOR CREATING CONTENT

Let's visit a few of these sites, compile a list of free press release sites, and add them to the list we compiled from Yahoo Answers. We can then sort them alphabetically, or however else we desire.

We'll also need to go through each one and ensure that they indeed offer free press release distribution.

That's really all there is to conducting research. Now, we just need to study our researched content, so we can write our own content based on the knowledge we've acquired. This may sound like a lot of work, but you will surprised how quickly this process happens.

There really isn't a hard and fast rule for how much content needs to be produced per chapter (topic). It really just depends on the niche and how much information is required to answer the why and how questions. The safe approach is to always over-deliver.

Now it's just a process of rinse and repeat. This procedure we just used to create content on *free advertising using press releases* is the same identical process we'll use to create content for the rest of our eBook's chapters.

8

THE INTERVIEW METHOD FOR CREATING CONTENT

Creating a Strategy for Conducting Interviews

As I stated earlier, conducting interviews has become a popular method for producing quality information products. In this chapter, we'll walk through each of the necessary steps to create an information product using the interview method.

First, we need to create a strategy, so that when we contact experts about setting up an interview, we can clearly communicate our plan.

For example, if we want to locate an expert on the topic of "press releases", then our strategy may look something like this:

THE INTERVIEW METHOD FOR CREATING CONTENT

Sample Interview Outline

Topic: Free Advertising Using Press Releases
Length of Interview: 30-45 Minutes
Agenda:

1. Introduction
2. Interview
   - How can writing press releases result in free website traffic?
   - What are the guidelines for writing a good press release?
   - Questions for expert from teleconference participants (optional)
   - What other tips or advice can you provide that would benefit an individual who is considering advertising using press releases?
   - Recap
   - Thank expert for his her time and advice.

As you can see in the example above, this is a simple strategy that lays out our interview, ensuring we cover all our bases. We need to repeat this process with our other topics i.e. forums, social networking sites, etc.

The ideal situation would be to locate experts who possess knowledge in two or more of these topics.

For example, if we could locate an expert who is knowledgeable and has achieved success with forum, social networking, blogging and press release advertising, this will obviously save time since we wouldn't need to interview as many experts. This shouldn't be very difficult to achieve since most successful internet marketers have achieved success due to their wealth of knowledge on various forms of website advertising.

There are several places we can search to find experts including blogs, forums, websites, and even outsourcing services. Let's take a look at these methods.

Finding Experts On Blogs

Out of all the methods for locating experts to interview, I personally believe that blogs are among the best places to search.

Bloggers are usually more accessible and easier to contact than website owners. Since blogs have so much content, it's relatively easy to assess a blogger's level of expertise.

To search blogs for experts, we'll conduct web searches using: "keyword+blog".

For example, if we search for an expert on social networking, we would type "social networking+blog" without the quotes.

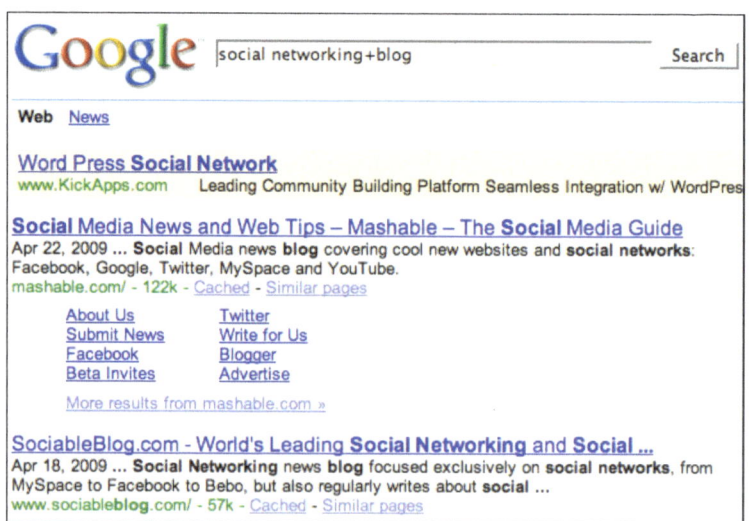

THE INTERVIEW METHOD FOR CREATING CONTENT

Now keep in mind that some of the blogs on Google's first page may have owners who are too busy to be interviewed.

That's OK, because there are many results from which to choose. It shouldn't be hard to locate experts who are willing to be interviewed.

Now as I mentioned earlier, the ideal situation would be to locate experts who possess expertise in *more* than one of our topics. To accomplish this, we would use more general keywords when conducting searches (e.g. website advertising+blog or internet marketing+blog, etc.).

Once we've identified a few blogs related to our topics, we need to qualify the blog owners before contacting them for interviews. This will ensure that the blog owners we contact are indeed knowledgeable and respected authorities on our topics. This is a relatively simple straightforward process and can be accomplished by answering the following questions:

- How many entries has the blog owner posted?

- How well are these entries written?
- What is the frequency of the posts (daily, weekly, etc.) and how recent is the current entry?
- Do the posts include comments from readers, and if so, is there a tone of respect expressed by commenters for the blogger? To find website owners who are experts on our topics we would simply replace the word "blog" with "website" when conducting searches (e.g. website advertising +website).

Finding Experts On Websites

Searching for experts on websites is very similar to the process used to find experts on blogs. The search is initiated the same way: "keyword+website.

To qualify website owners as experts on our topics we need to answer the following questions:

- How much relative content is on the website?
- Does the website include testimonials especially if it's a sales page?
- Is there contact information for the website owner?
- What is the Alexa ranking of the website? The benchmark should be 500,000 or less.

It's also a good idea to search the internet for information on the website's owner to see if there is favorable information or testimonials, which affirm him or her as an expert on the topic(s). This is accomplished by typing the website owner's name in a search engine using quotation marks (e.g., "John Doe").

Setting Up and Recording Interviews

This crucial step needs to be planned out well and tested

thoroughly. You certainly want to avoid any technical issues that would jeopardize your efforts and opportunity to conduct the interview(s).

You have two options for conducting the interview(s). You can keep it simple by only including you and the interviewee on the call or you can promote the interview and conduct it as a teleconference. The latter format allows for interaction with callers that breaks up the interview and allows for more variety and possible insight.

Conducting interviews using the teleconference format is viable if you and/or the interviewee already have a list of subscribers.

If you choose the teleconference route for your interview, you would need to communicate and organize this with the expert.

Let's take a look at what is required for both the simple interview method between you and the interviewee and the teleconference method.

The simple, two-party interview requires a calling service such as Skype.com, or a telephone and a means to record it. If you plan to use a telephone instead of Skype or a similar service, then you'll need to buy a telephone to PC adapter. I highly recommend Skype because it's cheap, reliable, and simple to use. To use Skype, simply download and setup their free software. Skype to Skype calls are free, so if an interviewee uses Skype also, you will incur no long distance fees. If the interviewee does not use Skype, you'll need to choose a payment method: pay as you go or pay monthly.

Once your account is set up, you'll need one more

mechanism in place to be ready to conduct the interview(s) which is the means to record the conversation. I highly recommend Stepvoice.com

This feature-rich software is relatively cheap, easy to use, and is downloadable to your computer. It also produces an MP3 of the recording that is the most compatible audio format.

The teleconference method requires only a telephone and use of a teleconference service. There are several services on the internet where you can host your teleconference. If you don't need a lot of "bells and whistles" and plan to have less than 96 people on the call, I highly recommend Freeconferencecall.com. Here's how the sign-up process works:

- Signup at Freeconferencecall.com.
- Check your email for details with instructions about your conference. You will receive a call-in number and pin number.
- Promote the teleconference to your subscribers and/ or ask the expert to promote to his or subscribers.

You will need to inform them of the teleconference's date, time, call-in telephone number, and pin number.

After the interview, you can receive an MP3 recording of it from Freeconferencecall.com. That's it! It's a very easy process.

Regardless of whether you use the simple interview method between you and the expert or decide to go the teleconference route, be sure to test the functionality and quality of the process thoroughly before the actual interview.

THE INTERVIEW METHOD FOR CREATING CONTENT

Transcribing Audio Into Text

Once you have the audio from your interview(s) or teleconference(s), you'll need to transcribe this into text. You have two options:

1. Do it yourself. If you intend to complete your product in 72 hours or less, I don't recommend this option. It is very time consuming, and you would be surprised how many words are in a 45-minute interview.

2. Outsource it. You can have audio transcribed into text relatively cheap by creating a project listing for this task on outsourcing websites such as Castingwords.com, Freelancer.com, etc.

If you go with the outsourcing option, I highly recommend the service, Castingwords.com. I have used them several times and have been quite pleased with the results and delivery time.

There is audio to text dictation software available, such as Dragon Naturally Speaking. This is certainly a viable option, however it will be a bit more expensive since you will need to purchase the software.

Outsourcing the Entire Process

If you want to produce an information product using the interview method but feel uncomfortable contacting experts or conducting interviews, you can outsource the entire process.

This option isn't cheap; however, if you can afford it, go

for it. Currently, Guru.com is the best place to outsource this process.

If you choose to outsource this process, you need to be certain that you are organized so you can clearly articulate the project in detail.

9

PACKAGING OPTIONS

Regardless of whether you choose the research method or the interview/teleconference method to create your product, you need to consider how to package your product. The way you package the product will depend on how you decide to deliver and price it.

Here are a few packaging options to consider:

Option 1: Text Only

This is the most popular method for packaging information products.

The .exe format used to be a popular format for compiling text, but there are major limitations with .exe files including their incompatibility with Macintosh computers.

Most all information products containing text are packaged into PDFs (portable document format).

Packaging information products such as eBooks into PDF's is very easy and can be accomplished using eBook compiling software or Adobe Acrobat Professional. It's pricy, but it's loaded with features.

Option 2: Audio Only

Use this option if wish to include audio only when selling your product. If you choose to create your information product using the interview/teleconference method, you can deliver your product in a basic MP3 format. Simply upload the MP3(s) on your web server and provide this web link to your customers so they can download the audio.

You can also burn your MP3(s) to CD, create a fancy label, and deliver it to your customers via mail. The advantages of selling your information product as a CD are the ability to charge more due to shipping and handling, supplies, etc., and having the residential addresses for your customer base. The obvious disadvantage is time, effort, and the extra resources required to burn and ship the CDs.

Option 3: Audio and Text

Use this option if you want to offer customers both audio and text versions of your information product.

Packaging both audio and text together allows you to sell your product as a higher ticket item since you are offering your customers more than one method for learning.

PACKAGING OPTIONS

If you decide to use the interview/teleconference method for creating your information product, simply transcribe your audio into text according to my instructions in Chapter 2 then your product is packaged and ready to sell.

If you decide to use the research method for creating your information product, you can still use this option by transcribing your text into audio. There are many types of applications that do this; however, much like the audio to text software, they currently are not suitable for our purposes. Therefore, this process needs to be done manually in order to achieve optimum results.

You can outsource this task, or do it yourself. If you have a decent speaking voice, you can do this quickly and easily using a cheap microphone and a free audio editing software such as Audacity (audacity.soundforge.net). I use Audacity often and I honestly believe that it is the best free software application I've ever used.

10

COMPILING YOUR EBOOK

Creating the Header and Footer

The first step in the process of compiling your eBook is to create the header and footer. Essentially, you are creating a template since every page will include the header and footer.

There is a twofold purpose of the header and footer: they create an appealing, aesthetic "look" for your product, and they're also a great place to include important information such as your website, product name and page numbers.

I have read more eBooks than I can begin to count and every one has it's own unique header and footer ranging from the very simple to the colorful and elaborate. It's really up to you, your level of creativity and honesty, and the type of product you're creating. In other words, your header and footer should complement your information product rather than taking away from it or creating a distraction. It's always better to create something clean and simple as opposed to gaudy and distracting.

Since there are no fixed rules regarding headers and footers, I won't spend too much time on this section. I personally like to create image graphics for my headers for aesthetic purposes and to make it easy for users to navigate from page to page and back to the table of contents. When I create this type of header, I keep the footer simple.

Creating the Title Page

The Title Page doesn't need to be fancy. If you have an e-cover, this is a good place to display it. If not, you can simply type your title.

You could also include a "thank you" to customers for buying your product and/or an invitation for customers to join your affiliate program or visit your blog.

To help you know specifically what should be on your title page, ask yourself the following question: What do I want my readers to know before they read my eBook? Although the title of your eBook should certainly be on the title page, the rest is totally up to you.

Creating the Table of Contents

The table of contents is usually on either the second or third page and provides readers with a snapshot of the eBook's contents.

The table of contents can be formatted in a variety of

ways; however, it should always include chapter titles and subtitles, if applicable.

If you follow the guidelines in this eBook, you can easily create your table of contents since you will already have the outline.

Considering the outline we created earlier for our "free advertising on the internet" product, all you would need to do is copy and paste the outline, create subtitles, add page references, and you're done.

In the example below, Press Releases is the title, the subtitles are below, and all include page numbers.

Creating the Legal Notice

It is important to include a legal notice with your information products. The legal notice discourages readers from making you liable for any damages done to them by what they construe as a result of information you've sold them. Accusations of damage or pain and suffering caused from an information product are rare; however, it is always better to be safe than sorry.

The legal notice should either be on the second page following your title page or on the page following your table of contents.

Creating the Resource Section

This is an optional section that is usually located at the end of eBooks. It should consist of a list of websites and resources that you feel would benefit the reader and compliment the information they've read in your eBook. For example, if you've provided instruction on a specific method for generating website traffic i.e. article marketing, you could include a link to a product which automates that traffic method (e.g., an article submitter).

If the sites you recommend have an affiliate program, join it and hyperlink the websites you recommend with your affiliate links.

Create the resource section by including the title of your resource, then underneath write a short description so your readers will know what it is and if it is something they want to buy. The only cautionary note I have regarding your eBook's resource section is to not include too many resources. One page is plenty of space to dedicate to this section.

Importing the Main Content

OK, we're almost there. Now you need to import all those articles written from the research you performed. It's just a matter of copying and pasting each section into your eBook then checking the format for proper page and paragraph breaks.

After your main content is laid out the way you want it, you'll need to type the page numbers for each item into your table of contents based on the section it corresponds to. Once you've completed this step, you're ready for the next step, Proofreading and Editing.

Creating Hyperlinks

The last step before proofreading is to hyperlink selected text. This would include references on your title page and in your main content and resource sections. You should also link each chapter title in the table of contents to their appropriate pages.

Selecting Fonts

Unfortunately, some eBook authors often ignore font selection. It is, however, necessary to choose a font that is legible and easy on the eyes. If you locate a font which is conducive to the theme of your eBook and that is easy to read, then you have a winning combination. You should never compromise readability for creativity though.

The way fonts are displayed in a text document differs from the way they appear once a document is converted to a PDF file. The reason is because the PDF is similar to an image. Therefore, words in a PDF file are not quite as crisp and clear as they are in a text format.

Typically, fonts that are light and somewhat plain work best in eBooks. Most thick fonts do not display clearly in PDF files and they usually appear somewhat blurry.

My favorite fonts to use in eBooks are:

- Gill Sans
- Quicksand (used in this eBook)
- Sans Serif fonts
- Georgia
- Times New Roman

COMPILING YOUR EBOOK

Proofreading and Editing

Proofreading and Editing your product is a very important and necessary step in compiling your eBook. An eBook full of grammatical errors reflects badly on the author and will certainly affect future sales.

If you're grammatically challenged like me, then you'll need to outsource this task. There are many great editing services on the internet. One that I highly recommend due to their quality service, speed, and value is Scribendi.com.

Converting to PDF

Once your eBook has been edited, the final step is converting your eBook into a PDF document. If you're a Mac user, this is no big deal since it already has a "save as PDF" feature built-in. If you're a PC user, then you'll need access to a PDF converter.

Free PDF converters have become quite popular and plentiful lately. You can easily find free converters online that allow you to upload text files then convert to PDF. Most of them will e-mail you the PDF file once the conversion process is complete.

One of the online services that I have used successfully is pdfonline.com. This site will convert your word document to PDF and email it you relatively fast.

As I previously stated, you also have the option of buying Adobe Acrobat Professional which will provide many options including securing your PDF. If you're just getting started with creating information products, I wouldn't fork out the cash to buy it. A free online converter will work fine.

11

FORMATTING AUDIO

Editing Audio Using Audacity

If you choose to package your information product in an audio format or include an audio file with your PDF file, you can clean up these files nicely using audio editing software.

My favorite audio editing software is Audacity (audacity.soundforge.net). It's free and is compatible with Macintosh and Windows-based computers. Audacity is simple to use and there are a plethora of user tutorials available online.

I recommend that you only perform a few specific steps in this process. If you attempt to do too much, you audio file(s) may not sound natural. Obviously, the degree of editing is determined by the quality of your raw, audio file.

Here's the process I follow when editing audio with Audacity:

FORMATTING AUDIO

- Open Audacity and upload audio file.
- Highlight waveform by clicking on "Edit", "Select", and "All".
- With the waveform highlighted, click on "Effects", "Amplifier", "Amplify", and "OK".
- Listen to audio to find extended dead space, annoying sounds or any other section you want to delete. Highlight these sections on waveform with cursor, click on "Edit" and "Delete".
- Finally, export to MP3 by clicking "File, "Export", then click on "Format" drop down menu and select "MP3 Files". Click "Save".

That's it! Be sure that you preview every action immediately after execution. This is important because you may not be satisfied with the results and need to undo.

12

PRICING YOUR PRODUCT

Since there are so many variables involved, I cannot advise you to set a *specific* price point for your product; however, I can provide a few tips to help you decide.

To get an idea about how to price your product, find similar products online to learn what these products offer and how they are priced.

Information products can be categorized as low-ticket, mid-ticket, high-ticket, and very high-ticket. Below are examples of each.

Low-Ticket
- Short reports between 12-15 pages.
- eBooks containing a compilation of information that is available free on the internet but is difficult and time-consuming to locate.
- Short audio clips

Mid-Ticket
- Short or medium-size eBooks containing information consisting of a new idea or revolutionary method for solving a problem.
- Large eBooks
- Information product on audio (CD or MP3 format)
- Paid membership sites

High Ticket
- Video Course on DVD
- Large eBooks packaged with CDs and/or DVDs
- Tele-seminar with Well-Known Expert

Very High Ticket
- Coaching/Mentoring

13

CONCLUSION

Congratulations on finishing this book. Now it's time to get busy creating your own information product. The longer you delay, the greater the chance you'll never begin.

The world will profit from your valuable information, and you will profit financially while experiencing the satisfaction of knowing that you've helped others.

www.ingramcontent.com/pod-product-compliance
Lightning Source LLC
Chambersburg PA
CBHW040853180526
45159CB00001B/414